KATE AND RANDY

Think About Food

from their Garden

From the "I Think" Series

Jacqueline H. Bull, Ph. D.

Leavitt Peak Press

ISBN: 978-1-969865-68-8 (sc)
ISBN: 978-1-969865-69-5 (e)

Rev. date: 12/10/2025

This book is dedicated to my parents
Gerry and Dan.

Also, dedicated to my grandparents
Kate, Joe, Agnes (nickname Randy) and Dan.

"Kate, Randy," calls Mommy, "Do you want to go to the food store with me?"

Kate and Randy shout together, "Can we pick out one treat?"

Kate and Randy run to the car. They are so happy it is almost summertime. The sun is making each day warmer. They do not have to put on coats like they do in the winter.

"Wow," says Randy, "what treat do I want today?"

Kate is looking out of the car window. She is thinking about her last treat. She got a bag of popcorn. Today, Kate thinks she does not want popcorn. Popcorn is good, but not for every food store treat. Kate thinks and thinks as she scratches her head. What do I want today?

"Wow! Look at all the different colors of food," says Kate.

Mommy tells them, "This is the part of grocery store that has so many fruits and vegetables."

"Kale!" Kate laughs. She sees the name kale on the sign. "That is almost my name. My name is K-a-t-e. Kale is k-a-l-e."

Randy rolls his eyes at Kate. He does not think this is funny.

Randy sees a box of really big watermelons on the floor. He thinks the watermelons must be special to get so big and have a box just for them.

Kate and Randy see the red tomatoes. And in different sizes!

On the way home from the store, Kate and Randy eat their treat. Oatmeal raisin cookies!

After dinner, Daddy, Kate, and Randy go into their backyard. Daddy says, "Let's dig some holes!"

"Play in the dirt, really?" shouts Randy.

"Yes," says Daddy. "We are going to plant our own tomato plants. When they grow, we can pick the tomatoes and eat them."

Kate likes tomatoes in salads and sometimes in a sandwich with lettuce and bread. She is so happy.

Randy is happy to get to dig holes and get dirty.

On the ground next to the holes they are digging are green plants. Kate thinks each plant looks like a green drinking straw with green leaves on top.

Kate and Randy remember the tomatoes they saw in the grocery store. How can a green plant make a red tomato?

Randy sits on the ground next to the plants. He laughs. "The tomato plants are the same size as my sneakers."

Daddy says, "In a few weeks, the plants will be as tall as the two of you. And each plant will grow red tomatoes."

Kate and Randy help Daddy dig holes in the dirt. They place one plant in each hole. Then they put the dirt back in the ground around the plant. This will make the plant stand tall.

Every day, Kate and Randy look to see if the tomato plants are getting taller. They are! And some of the plants have little yellow flowers.

Randy keeps looking at the plants that are almost as tall as he is. He scratches his head and wonders, How did the plants grow so fast? What used to be the size of my sneakers are now as tall as me. And now the yellow flowers are green balls! What is going on?

One morning, Mommy and Daddy hear Kate and Randy laughing. Mommy and Daddy wonder what is going on!

Kate and Randy are shouting, "We have red tomatoes. We grew our very own tomatoes. Wow! We grew red tomatoes!" Kate and Randy jump up and down. "Can we have them for breakfast? Can we?"

Mommy and Daddy run into the backyard a few steps behind their children. As they look at the plants, Mommy and Daddy say they have to let the tomatoes stay on the plants for a few more days.

"Each day the round ball tomatoes will get bigger, and the red color will get brighter. Just think," says Mommy, "the bigger the red tomatoes grow, the more we will have to eat."

Kate and Randy together jump up and down and laugh as they sing, "We helped make our special treats. We helped the green plants grow.

Mommy says, "We are going to be eating tomatoes from our garden all summer."

"Yippeee!" shout Kate and Randy. They just wish it was time to start eating them now!

Mommy, Daddy, Kate, and Randy all laugh as they hear birds chirping.

"Wow," says Randy. "A lot is going on in our backyard."

It seems like, days and days, before Mommy tells Kate and Randy that it is time to pick some tomatoes.

Then, one day, Mommy calls Kate and Randy to join her in the backyard. Mommy walks to the tomato plants. She picks a tomato. Then she looks at Kate and Randy and asks, "Did you see how I gently pulled the tomato from the plant? We do not want to shake the plants and have all the tomatoes fall to the ground."

With a smile on her face, Mommy asks Kate and Randy, "Would you like to pick a tomato?"

Mommy points to two tomatoes. She says, "I think these tomatoes will be really good in the salad we are going to have with dinner tonight."

Kate and Randy finally get to pick a tomato!

While sitting at the dinner table, Daddy says, "I am really hungry, and I know our tomatoes will taste so good."

Daddy puts dinner food on Kate's and Randy's plates.

"Don't forget the salad," says Randy. "Tonight I am going to eat my salad first. I know the tomato on my plate is the one I picked."

Randy thinks as he asks, "Daddy, does this mean I am a farmer like the one in our storybook?"

Daddy looks at Randy and says, "Yes, son. You grew tomatoes just like the farmers who grow the tomatoes in the grocery store. Just think about the big backyard the farmer has. Big enough to grow so many tomatoes and all the other fruits and vegetables you see in the grocery store."

Randy's eyes get really big, and he shouts, "Farmers have a really big backyard!"

Daddy asks Kate and Randy, "Would you like to grow tomatoes and other vegetables in our garden next summer?"

Kate and Randy did not say anything.

This surprises Daddy. "What is wrong? asks Daddy. "Did you have fun working in the garden?"

Kate looks at her parents and says, "Let me think! What vegetable do I want to grow next summer?"

All of a sudden Kate shouts out, "I know, corn!"

Mommy and Daddy shout, "Corn! Why do you want to grow corn?"

"So I can make popcorn," says Kate. "Sometimes I like my grocery store treat to be popcorn. With corn in our garden, I can have popcorn and don't have to go to the grocery store. It will be in our backyard, just like the tomatoes."

Randy was not saying anything. This surprises both Mommy and Daddy. What is Randy thinking?

Mommy asks Randy, "Tell us what you would like to grow in our garden next summer."

Randy looks at Mommy, Daddy, and Kate. Then he says, "I want to grow watermelons!"

"Watermelons!" Everyone laughs.

"Why do you want to grow watermelons?" ask Daddy.

Mommy, Daddy, and Kate did not think Randy would pick watermelons.

Randy smiles and says, "In the grocery store, watermelons get a special box on the floor since they are too big to be on the shelves with the other fruits and vegetables. If I eat watermelons, I know I am going to be big and strong and special!"

Activity Page

To cut a tomato for a salad, place the tomato on a plate. Cut the top of the tomato off if there are some flowers from the plant. Cut the tomato in half. Then cut the two pieces of the tomato in half. The tomato will now be in four pieces that can be in a salad.

To cut a tomato for a sandwich, place the tomato on a plate. Cut the top of the tomato off if there are some flowers from the plant. Cut the tomato in thin slices from the top all the way to the end. Place the slices of tomato in your sandwich!

www.ingramcontent.com/pod-product-compliance
Lightning Source LLC
Chambersburg PA
CBHW042344030426
42335CB00030B/3456